Become an
Appointment
Machine
In One Day

Second Edition

by
R. Grant Baker
J.T. Tasker

Meer Press
New York

Cover art by
J.R.FISHWORKS

To our family and friends
who have supported us through the years.
Without their inspiration
this book would not have been written.

Contents

In the mind of a prospect,
your company's image and value
is either confirmed or redefined,
for better or for worse,
within the first few seconds
of your approach.

— J.T. TASKER / R. GRANT BAKER

Introduction

PROSPECTING, CANVASSING, COLD CALLING, generating new business — no matter what phrase you use, these words strike fear and frustration into the hearts and minds of many unsuccessful, as well as, astonishingly enough, many "successful" sales professionals. Sales reps often avoid it, sales managers wish their people were better at it, and senior management does not understand what the big deal is.

Perhaps you have found yourself with your prospect list in hand and with the best of intentions to set the world on fire, yet staring at the phone was the only thing you accomplished that day. Or maybe you have fearlessly burned through a quality prospect list, but your calendar is still bare. If so, then The Appointment Machine™ was written for you.

A company can spend whatever sum of money it wants on research and development, superior infrastructure, and the all-important investments in advertising and promoting their "brand image" — telling the world about its great and unique value. But if that company's sales reps avoid prospecting or, worse yet, repel would-be clients as a result of poor skills, then all the above-mentioned investments of resources will be at best under-utilized, or, worse yet, wasted completely. This book was written with the acute and vital understanding that a company's image is "redefined" in the mind's eye of a prospect, for better or worse, within the first few seconds of a sales rep's approach.

The rewards of a successful sales career are almost too many to count. In addition to being among the highest-paid professionals in today's workforce, successful sales representatives enjoy many benefits beyond just high compensation. They also are sought after by companies large and small, respected by their customers, and admired by co-workers and management alike. For you to enjoy these benefits, performance is all that stands in your way.

So why doesn't everyone who enters a sales career achieve success? What is it that separates the performers from the non-performers? Could it be that they are smooth talkers, well-connected, fearless, slick, polished and quick on their feet? Do they have the best territories, work night and day, and maybe, just maybe, are smarter than the rest of the team? The answer is no.

The truth is that top performers are pretty much like everyone else. They do have one unique trait, though — one difference that separates them from the rest: their consistent ability to be in front of qualified prospects more often than everyone else.

Top performers spend more time in front of prospects who are interested in their product or service and who are in a position to do business with them. They are constantly meeting with decision-makers and moving the sales cycle forward, all the while adding to their working list of prospects. They have mastered the ability to set appointments with new, qualified prospects. They know how to create momentum. They are, in effect, Appointment Machines.

Before we move on, let's define the term prospecting. We believe that prospecting is defined as **the process of contacting prospective clients to identify if they are qualified for, and open to an appointment for the purpose of beginning a sales cycle.**

Effective and efficient prospecting requires the following:

1. **Initiating contact with prospective customers in a way that differentiates you from others.**

The first contact made with a prospective customer or client must be positive, and becomes the foundation upon which your business relationship will be built. Therefore, it is critical that your company's unique and specific value is communicated clearly, concisely and in a way that your prospect will hear it.

2. **Assessing an appropriate action consistent with the prospect's buying schedule.**

Knowing a prospect's timetable to make a decision is key to properly investing your time. Once prospects are identified, having an acute understanding of their time-to-buy schedule gives you the ability to properly prioritize your most valuable asset — your time.

3. **Gaining permission to begin a sales cycle, or to stay in touch.**

A prospect who finds value in exploring a relationship with you and your company will allow future contact as a normal course of business. However, if the timing of your initial call is not appropriate, staying in regular contact with your prospect is essential to ensuring that you, your product and your company are able to compete for the business when the time is right.

4.   **Keeping accurate records.**

Over time, your prospecting calls will generate valuable information. This includes contact names, addresses, phone numbers, current vendors, contract expirations, needs, goals, state of business, interest level, change in management or buyer, as well as the most recent objection or what we refer to as "Pushback". Not taking the time to record this information is a "crime" against your company and a "crime" against your future earnings. Accurate records of your prospecting efforts will save you time and definitely make you money.

We believe that prospecting done right and done consistently is what separates the top performers from the rest.

Not convinced? OK, then do this: Go to the most successful sales rep you know and ask to look at that rep's personal calendar for the last 90 days. Chances are good that each day's schedule will show that the rep was either on an appointment or doing what is necessary to set more appointments. Without question, if you present your product or service to a greater number of qualified prospects, it is safe to say that success will follow. That is what becoming an Appointment Machine is all about — taking the guesswork out of prospecting and in turn creating enthusiasm and confidence in setting appointments with qualified prospects.

Using professional sports as an analogy, top-level athletes, without exception and regardless of the sport, started their careers by learning and then perfecting the fundamentals. What is often overlooked, though, is that even after reaching professional status, these athletes continue to practice the basics. We would all be hard-pressed to think of one professional athlete who does not start each season by going over and over the fundamental skills that were first learned years, if not decades ago. Whether it be Tiger Woods on the driving range or Serena Williams practicing her serve, it seems that no mater how advanced they become, the truly great athletes still rely on the fundamentals.

Professional sales is no different. Success comes from the consistent application of field-tested fundamentals. The quicker you master setting appointments and truly become an Appointment Machine, the quicker success will follow.

How to Use This Book
Because we as sales people are impatient by nature, we constructed this book so that in one day or less anyone who is truly focused can learn all that is required. Anyone who puts the principles contained in the following chapters into their daily routine will undoubtedly rise to top-performer status.

Who Can Benefit From This Book?
Becoming an Appointment Machine is just as important to new sales reps just getting started in their territory and wanting to get out of the gate quickly as it is for the more experienced sales reps who want to re-energize their career. Setting business appointments is also important to new business owners who need

to venture out of the office to promote their business face to face with prospects.

This book is designed to be your workbook, with plenty of spaces to take notes, create and test scripts, and organize your success plan. We first address some of the common reasons why so many sales people hesitate to prospect. Once you remove the hesitation barrier, you will be free to go forward and develop new appointment-setting skills, or sharpen rusty ones. Once action and skill are put into motion, the resulting momentum will be profitable, fun and hard to stop. Follow each step to the letter, and you will find that you have a new attitude about prospecting. You'll be waist-deep in appointments as your bank account begins to show the results.

Start now.

Your First Few Seconds Exercise

Prospecting — either in person, at a trade show or via the telephone — requires that you capture the attention and interest of your prospect. Assume for a moment that you are prospecting one of us (the authors) to set an appointment to promote your product or service. Write your approach dialogue in the space provided below. It is important that you write down **exactly** what you say to a new prospect, up to the point that you begin to qualify them for your offering.

You will be asked to return to this page from time to time throughout the book. We recommend that you use a pencil for this exercise.

(Do not read any further until you have finished the exercise.)

_____

_____

_____

_____

_____

_____

_____

_____

Twenty years from now
you will be more
disappointed by the things you didn't do
than by the ones you did do.
So throw off the bow lines.
Sail away from the safe harbour.
Catch the trade winds in your sails.
Explore. Dream. Discover.

— MARK TWAIN

1

What Holds You Back and Pushes Your Prospects Away?

YOU MAY HAVE HEARD PEOPLE SAY, "I know that my prospects would be as excited as I am if only they knew how great this product or service is. If I could only get the appointment, I know they would buy from me."

Nothing could be truer. Your excitement and commitment can be infectious when prospects get the opportunity to see it. However, for them to see it, you need to set the appointment. Other than just plain old-fashioned laziness, we believe **there are only two** reasons for a general lack of appointments:

- #1: Avoiding prospecting due to lack of self-confidence or fear of rejection — what we call **contact hesitation**.

- #2: The lack of specific appointment-setting **skills** — knowing what to say and how to say it.

Hesitation

Have you ever found yourself less than enthusiastic about contacting that next prospect? Well, you are not alone. Contact hesitation wreaks havoc on many a sales professional — both new and seasoned alike. Some of us are just uncomfortable with picking up the phone to make prospecting calls, or simply walking up to someone we do not know and introducing ourselves. This condition is normal for many, but when this condition exists within a person who has chosen sales as a career, it is oftentimes assumed that the salesperson either is lazy, has poor work habits or is unskilled.

Skill
On the other end of the spectrum, there are the fearless ones who don't hesitate one bit. They can burn through a prospect list or shake hands with everyone in a room in no time. However, if they lack basic skills, they can either turn a great prospect list into a worthless pile of paper, or repel a flock of would-be qualified prospects. In turn, they often end up discouraged and defeated, and begin looking for alternative career opportunities.

Does this sound like anyone you know? You, perhaps? Never fear — the **Appointment Machine** is here to help you:

1. Remove all reasons for hesitating to make initial contact with any prospect, and
2. Develop razor-sharp prospecting skills.

Hesitation Revealed
Public television recently aired a documentary on the Bengal tiger in India. Impressive was the strength, grace and confidence the tiger projected as it mastered its domain. This documentary sadly detailed how these magnificent animals are hunted for sport. Before the hunt begins, a clearing is prepared by unrolling a 5-foot-tall strip of cheesecloth around the perimeter, leaving one side open for the tiger to enter.

Meanwhile, a group of men with high-powered rifles ride atop several elephants. The men enter a part of the forest where a tiger is believed to be sleeping. Running alongside the elephants are several other men with drums and sticks. Their goal is to make enough noise to scare the tiger out of its home and toward the clearing, where more hunters await.

Once the tiger enters the clearing, two men hiding in the trees stretch more cheesecloth across the opening, trapping the tiger inside a cheesecloth cage.

To the tiger, the cheesecloth might just as well be a 30-foot-tall brick wall. The hunters celebrate as the tiger experiences a paralyzing fear, running around the perimeter looking for an opening. As the frantic tiger looks for a way out, a single bullet ends the hunt.

We all know that the tiger could have escaped with little or no difficulty. It could have easily ripped through the cheesecloth or simply jumped over it. In fact, the tiger was never physically trapped at all. The tiger was trapped only by its ***perception*** that the cheesecloth was an inescapable barrier — not by the barrier itself. This false perception caused the tiger to hesitate long enough for fear to take over. It was this fear that gave the cheesecloth the power to enslave the tiger.

Similar to the tiger in the story, sales professionals can be trapped by their own cheesecloth cages. A negative perception can distort truth, giving life and power to fear. Fear, no matter its cause, can kill action. Lack of action in the form of prospecting will limit the exposure of your business, products, ideas and/or services to others, and in turn limit your success. One does not need a Ph.D.

in psychology to understand the stranglehold that **contact hesitation** can have on productivity.

The first step to becoming an **Appointment Machine** is to change the perceptions that may cause you to hesitate. Our objective is to remove this fear so that it no longer can hold your actions hostage. In fact, this new insight will actually fuel positive thoughts so that rather than you being hesitant, you will be hard-pressed to hold back your enthusiasm as you reach for the phone or extend your hand to introduce yourself, your company, your product, your service and your value to the next prospect.

It has been said that *action cures fear*. You know, the just-get-out-there-and-do-it mentality. Perhaps it is true for some that action alone will win over fear. But what happens to the person who is too afraid to act? If fear is preventing someone from getting started, what then?

If we had been given this "just do it" counsel during our first disastrous attempts in the sales field, we never would have written this book. We never would have had a track record of success to draw from. Without a doubt, we both acknowledge that we would have been too hesitant to act. Our performance would have suffered, and we would have either sought, or been forced to seek, different lines of work.

Sharpen Your Skills
There once was a lumberjack who walked into a camp looking for work. To prove he was the best lumberjack the foreman had ever seen, he boasted that he could chop down more trees than anyone

in the history of the company. Given the chance to prove himself, the lumberjack set out for the woods bright and early with the goal of chopping down 10 trees that day. As the story goes, he only felled nine trees the first day, tying the previously established record. With stern determination he set out to beat the record on the second day, but he only felled seven trees. On day three, while putting in just as many hours, his production fell again, with only five trees hitting the ground.

I have never worked so hard and gotten so little done, the lumberjack thought to himself. *I don't understand it.* On the fourth day, he set out for the woods an hour earlier than the three days before. The foreman stopped him just as he left camp. "I notice you are working pretty hard and getting less and less done. What do you think is wrong?" he asked. "I don't know," said the lumberjack. "I have never worked so hard and not hit my goals. I guess I just need to work harder."

With a big smile, the foreman said, "I know you've been busy, but in the past few days, have you taken the time to sharpen your axe?"

Well, you guessed it — the lumberjack had not sharpened his axe since he first set out to break the record. In fact, he came to the camp with a dull axe. Without knowing it, the odds were stacked against him. The dull axe he held in his hands limited his productivity and kept him from his goal. It is also important to note that the harder he worked without reaching his goal, the more **frustrated** and **discouraged** he became.

Let's apply this story to the proper and productive way to make prospecting contacts. For example, it's likely you have used the phone at least once on every day you can ever remember. Without even thinking about it, you have picked up the phone, dialed a number and heard the familiar ring, and if a live voice answers, a conversation begins. Not a big deal, is it? Also, it is safe to assume that you have at one time or another been introduced to someone you did not know. Without too much trouble and anxiety, you have looked this stranger in the eye, extended your hand, said "How do you do?" and shaken hands. This is not a big deal either, is it?

Without realizing it, over the years you have developed some basic contacting skills as well as some basic interpersonal social skills. However, proactively using the phone to make a business contact or introducing yourself to a prospect requires new skills. Going forward without first taking the time to learn these skills and master them is just like our lumberjack friend setting out to do a job carrying an unsharpened axe.

Everyone, regardless of experience level, can benefit from sharper, more precise contacting skills. It is true that an average sales professional who puts in the effort and represents a good product can survive with average prospecting skills. We assume that you would not be reading this book if your sights are set on "average." The truth is, your prospects have been bombarded with approach after approach by sales reps trying to gain their attention. Like the homeowner who lives near railroad tracks and no longer pays attention to or "hears" the trains that repeatedly scream by, a prospect can become "numb" to the common approach. The problem is that to the prospect, we as sales professionals all "sound" the same, and as such can easily be tuned out.

Sharpening your prospecting skills is as important to the sales professional as a sharp axe is to the lumberjack.

Would you rather work with a sharp axe, make progress and be excited with the results, or work really hard with a dull axe and make little progress, with the best you can hope for being "average" performance? It doesn't sound like a difficult question, but picking up the phone or walking up to a stranger for the sole purpose of setting an appointment without first sharpening the *right skills* is much like trying to set the all-time tree-felling record and only having a dull axe to use.

This is why one person can invest an hour on the phone and set up enough appointments to last the entire week, and be enthused and excited about the week ahead. Meanwhile, another can spend that same hour working with undeveloped skills, get nowhere and become discouraged. Such people feel as if they are spinning their wheels. They begin to doubt their business, their product and their abilities — never reaching their full potential.

Defeating **contact hesitation** and sharpening new contacting **skills** is all that stands between you and success.

Progress is the activity
of today and the
assurance of tomorrow.

— RALPH WALDO EMERSON

2

Defeat Contact Hesitation Once and For All

IN THIS CHAPTER WE ARE GOING TO TAKE A CLOSER LOOK at the forces that give life to contact hesitation. We believe that understanding the roots of these thoughts is the first step to defeating them.

Remembering how, in Chapter One, the tiger was trapped by its perception that the flimsy cheesecloth couldn't be broken, we can imagine what would have happened if that same group of hunters found themselves eye to eye with a tiger that knew its cage was only cheesecloth.

What if the tiger knew that this was an attempt on its life, its freedom and its family? Imagine for a moment that the same tiger had entered the clearing and saw the white cheesecloth, yet had been there before and understood that the wall of white before him was a paper-thin barrier put there by men who wanted to frighten, confuse and ultimately kill him.

Imagine what would happen if at that critical moment, the weakness of the cheesecloth was revealed to the trapped tiger. Picture the change in the tiger's posture — a movement from fear to anger, a newfound attitude of strength and confidence that only a moment before reflected fear and confusion.

Imagine the look in the tiger's eye as it realizes that there is nothing to be afraid of. Free from the false perception that could have held it hostage, the empowered tiger would **without hesitation** break through to freedom, never to be trapped again!

Contact Hesitation — It's Normal

Dealing with a new situation can be uncomfortable for anyone. Making business contacts may be a new experience for you, so relax — it's normal to feel those butterflies. Most everyone who has used the phone to set appointments, or walked right past the "No Soliciting" sign in an office building, has experienced contact hesitation. For some it's just an annoyance, a momentary feeling of discomfort. For others, this uneasy feeling of hesitation turns into all-out, paralyzing fear.

The fears that result in contact hesitation are fueled by our thoughts and perceptions. It is **how we think** that causes hesitation and limits our success. The bad news is that many of us have thought this way for most of our professional lives. The good news is that we **can** control how we think and change it for the better.

We can choose to think differently, think positively and think right! In developing a new way of thinking, we can come to the understanding that there is really nothing to be afraid of. In fact, there is a lot to be excited about, to look forward to, and to enthusiastically share with others..

Let us first say that we are not psychologists. We speak from the point of view of sales professionals who have experienced these fears firsthand and who have spent years studying why setting appointments is such a difficult skill for so many to master.

We believe it boils down to this: Most, if not all fears relating to contact hesitation are rooted in the **negative anticipation** of **"What will they think?"**

We all care in varying degrees about how we are perceived by others. We are especially concerned with how we are perceived by those we love, respect or believe have a higher status in life. It is our choice to believe whether we, or our approach, are perceived positively or negatively by others.

People with a negative anticipation of "What will they think?" believe that those they call on don't want to be bothered and don't need what they are offering, and they believe that their prospects think that they are only interested in making the sale, getting their money and moving on.

People with a **positive anticipation** of **"What will they think?"** believe that their prospects will be glad that they called and need what they have to offer, and believe that they are looking out for their prospects' well-being.

I (Grant) remember going through some old files that a former sales rep had left before moving on to another assignment. One file was labeled in big, bold, red letters: ***The rudest man I have ever dealt with. Don't bother***.

By this time, my sales career was on a roll. I was making business contacts comfortably and setting appointments at will. Looking through the file, it appeared that the prospect had evaluated our products about a year before and had decided to stay with a competitor's equipment. Looking further into the file, I learned that he was the decision-maker for not one, not two, but six pieces of production equipment representing almost half my semiannual quota.

Knowing the competition as I did, I knew deep down that he couldn't be that happy with his current situation, so I picked up a script I had developed for these types of calls and dialed his direct line. Fully expecting him to be as rude to me as he had been to the last guy, I listened to the ringing phone while thinking to myself, This should be interesting. The conversation went something like this:

Grant: *"John Smith, my name is Grant Baker from Eastman Kodak's Copy Products Division. We have not met yet, but I believe you spent some time with Jim Mathews evaluating our duplicating equipment. I know you are busy — do you have just a few moments?"*

Mr. Smith: *"What did you say your name was?"*

Grant: *"Grant Baker with..."*

Mr. Smith: *(cutting me off... he really was rude)*
"Yes, yes, with Eastman Kodak's Copy Products. I know, I know ... I'm listening."

Grant: *"Great, the reason why I'm calling is to ask for a bit of your time to introduce myself and acquaint you with some of our new products. What days this week are you tied ..." (I can't believe it. He cut me off again.)*

Mr. Smith: *"Stop by tomorrow at 10:00."*

Grant: *"Terrific, 10:00 at your office on University Ave."*

Mr. Smith: *"No, I have moved my office to Union Square; 22 Union Square, fifth floor."*

Grant: *"Glad I confirmed. I am writing in my calendar 10:00 tomorrow at your office on the fifth floor of 22 Union Square."*

Click. (He hung up on me. He really was the rudest man I had ever met. He never said goodbye.)

As it turned out, when I met Mr. Smith that next morning, he needed what I had to offer. He was glad I called, and over the next several years he became one of my best customers. In fact, he often offered himself as a reference and gladly recommended my products (in his own rude way) to anyone who asked.

This all took place because I chose to have a positive anticipation of "what Mr. Smith would think." I knew if he had our products, he would be happy. I knew he would be better off dealing with me than with the competition. I knew it. I believed it. And because I was so sure, I did not hesitate to make the contact and set the appointment.

You might be thinking, *That's nice, but what if this Mr. Smith guy didn't want to see you? What if he was not interested? What if you took action and did not win this time? What then?* We can answer that with one single word: NEXT! I just saved myself some time.

I still believe I have the best product and service to offer. If Mr. Smith or anyone else is not ready to hear about it, that does not change the fact that I believe what I offer is of value.

Turn Hesitation Into Enthusiasm

Answer this question quickly without thinking about it. Would you call your neighbor at 3:30 a.m.? No! Why not? Is it because they might not want to be bothered? Perhaps they might think poorly of you? Maybe your call would not be welcomed? But how about this: What if your neighbor's house was on fire? Do you think your neighbor would mind a call from you then? Do you think your call would be considered an intrusion, or do you think maybe, just maybe, your neighbor would be glad you called?

This example may be a bit extreme, but the point is the same: If you **believe** you have a compelling reason to call, then you **will not hesitate!** Calling someone is not a big deal as long as you have something important to discuss and have something of value to offer.

For me it was easy. I had compelling reasons why someone would want to meet with me. These compelling reasons were clear in my mind. And I believed them. In short, my perception was, **"Who wouldn't want to hear about my great equipment?"** I believed without a doubt that a prospect who needed my type of equipment would value my benefits. They would be able to enjoy these benefits only after they knew about them. And it was up to me to tell them.

What are your reasons to call your prospects? Do you know these reasons by heart? What is it about your offerings that will bring prospects happiness or somehow enhance their personal or professional lives? And here's the real question: Do **you believe it?** Believing that you are calling with something that can make others happy or in some way enhance their lives gives you the "**power of positive anticipation**." Your mind switches from "I might be bothering them" to "I bet they will be glad I called!"

There is a lot of "psychobabble" published by some really smart people who in 400-plus pages can tell you in detail about every prospecting-related fear you could imagine: fear of failure, fear of rejection, fear of self-promotion, and on and on. The reality is, that cause of contact hesitation is no more complex than the **negative** *anticipation* of "**What will they think?**" So from this point on, we won't bore you with any other reasons for you or anyone else to be afraid to initiate contact with a new prospect. Trust us — it is no more complicated that this.

Believe that your prospects:
- Will be glad that you called.
- Need what you have to offer.
- Know that you are looking out for their well-being.

Internalizing your value to your prospect is a major step toward developing an impenetrable shield against Contact Hesitation. This requires developing a belief system that says, "What I have is of great value, I am the best partner my client could have, my price is right, my prospects need what I offer, and any client working with me is fortunate."

When you believe this, you will have this hesitation thing licked. Bottom line — end of story.

Value Exercise I

Take a moment and think of the top benefits your prospects stand to enjoy should they decide to see you. In short, describe the value they will receive when they become a customer or client of yours. Write them in the spaces provided under the column labeled "My Value." Use only the space provided on the left column; leave the column on the right blank. We will use these values later on as we begin to build custom dialogue in Chapter Four. Do not go forward until you have completed this exercise. Much of the progress you will make begins here.

My Value	

A sales rep who fails to be empathetic
to a prospect's concerns, business issues or ideas
will struggle for each and every appointment.

— J.T. TASKER / R. GRANT BAKER

3

Differentiate Yourself at "Hello" with STEER™

WHILE PRACTICING LAW IN SPRINGFIELD, ILLINOIS, Abraham Lincoln developed an effective technique to give himself an edge over the opposition when trying a case. Lincoln gave great thought to the feelings, ideas and perspectives of the opposing legal team. *If I were representing the other side, he thought, what would I be thinking? How would I prepare to defeat me, the opposing legal team? What would my key arguments be? What evidence would I present? Where was the common ground? Where would I see weakness in my case?*

Lincoln saw the value in seeing things from another's perspective; that is, taking the time to be empathetic of the opposition. He found this practice to be of great advantage. Along with his strong work ethic, having a keen sense of empathy made Abraham Lincoln one of the finest lawyers of the day.

Prospect Empathy™

In the business and sales arena, we have coined a term for this prepared insight: **Prospect Empathy**. Becoming an **Appointment Machine** takes more than knowing your product from top to bottom. In the past you may have found yourself running through a shopping list of your product's or service's features, hoping by chance that you might stumble over the one that most interested your prospect. All the time you felt like you were trying to climb a greased pole, never confident that you were getting any closer to your desired goal.

Prospect Empathy encompasses both a mindset as well as a well-conceived, tactfully strategic, constructive inquiry into a prospect's state of fairness, desire for outside ideas and solutions, openness to input, and openness to options and/or change.

The importance of having empathy for your potential customer cannot be overstated. Here's a case in point: Americans are often comfortable with and respect "straight talk" or "telling it like it is"; however, to the Japanese this style of language, posture and tone is perceived as negative and offensive. Without this prepared understanding, or Prospect Empathy, a potentially lucrative business relationship could be derailed before it ever has a chance to be put in motion.

It is not uncommon for senior executives of U.S. corporations to be coached at great expense on the ways, customs and business practices of their foreign prospects. Prospect Empathy is often the difference between the success and failure of international business relationships. If it is worth the time and effort for one executive to go to "charm school" to re-learn how to address a foreign counterpart, it is well worth your time to cultivate empathy for the business issues facing your prospect.

We are not implying that, for example, one would need to take an accounting course in order to effectively sell to CPAs and accountants. We are saying, however, that the probability that a CPA would take the time to meet with a sales professional increases when the sales representative takes the time to research or at least consider the unique aspects of a CPA's business. The sales professional must ask, "What are the competitive pressures, day-to-day operational concerns, client-base issues and other factors that affect the day-to-day running of their businesses?"

Prospect Empathy helps you understand what it is like to be your prospect, and then, based on that understanding, tailor your prospecting dialogue for maximum results. It is more than just being aware of and sensitive to the variety of activities, responsibilities, priorities and business issues on the minds of your prospects. Prospect Empathy implies that this understanding becomes the cornerstone for developing your prospecting strategy.

For example, assume for a moment that your target prospects are independent grocery-store managers, and your job is to convince them to carry your product on their shelves. A typical approach might center on the money that the store will make on each of your products purchased from the prospect's store. Or it might focus on the high margin per transaction, or on how your return and stocking policies are the best in the industry. Sounds good, doesn't it? But what may really be on the minds of managers is the fact that Wal-Mart is now the No. 1 mover of groceries in the country and is seriously cutting into their customer base.

A more empathetic approach might be to show that your product is of local interest with limited distribution, thus inappropriate for the shelves of a Wal-Mart. A customer who wants the product will find it only on the shelves of the prospect's independent store. That way the prospect can bring back loyal customers by offering products that the consumer wants but are unavailable in any superstore.

Sales professionals with Prospect Empathy use every bit of

information about their prospects — including the prospects' industry, economic climate, and competitive pressures and strategies — to make their approach distinct.

Develop the Advantage of Prospect Empathy

There are several sources of information to help develop empathy for prospects and their industry's unique characteristics and current needs. The first, and perhaps most valuable, of these sources is a current customer or client. Ask current customers to describe what occupies their day, using simple questions like, "What are the top three issues you are dealing with right now that consume your mental energies?" or "What are the top reasons that you chose to become a customer of our company, and why did you buy from me when you did?" (timing and value). Once you ask these types of questions, have your pen and paper ready and take notes. You will walk away with several clues as to what may be on the minds of many other prospects.

Other sources that you may find valuable in developing Prospect Empathy are:

Economic information
- Internet
- Library
- Newspaper (local business section)
- *Wall Street Journal*
- Industry information
- Trade journals
- Trade publications
- Industry associations
- Association Web sites

Local business information
- Local business journal
- Business directories
- Chamber of Commerce newsletters

Identifying trends that affect your prospects' business is another powerful tool that displays to your prospects that you can be a valuable business partner offering great value in their efforts to improve the day-to-day operation of their businesses. Trends to consider are sales volume, competition (offshore and local), government regulations, changes in tax law, company expansion and/or downsizing, competitors' expansion and/or downsizing, industry consolidation, shifts in technology and how they affect their business, and so on. Can you think of more trends and how they may affect your prospects' customer base? Write them down and commit them to memory!

Prospect Empathy helps you realize that prior relationships may have been developed between current suppliers and the buyer, and that those bonds, and the comfort level that can accompany them, can be strong and must be respected if they are ever to be overcome. Effective sales reps understand that **status quo** is their biggest competition (**status quo** will be discussed in greater detail in Chapter 7). They discover that their products and services don't just sell themselves, nor are they often being sought after by their prospects. As a matter of fact, they may be the **last** thing on the prospects' mind when they are interrupted by your call.

Prospect Empathy is gained through dialogue that is designed to respectfully evaluate a prospect's authority to make decisions, as well as discover the prospect's degree of satisfaction with the current supplier's level of service, product quality, performance, warranty and/or value. Prospect Empathy encourages the use of the right words in the right tone at the right time to the right people. It is a powerful tool in the development of effective appointment-setting dialogue.

In addition, Prospect Empathy involves forethought and preparation. Sales representatives with Prospect Empathy embrace the reality that their offerings may not be appropriate for every prospect. This is achieved through a professional posture resulting from an attitude that reflects a belief that the sales professional's role is that of an equal. In other words, you offer potential clients a business partnership with great mutual benefit.

Value Exercise II
Now that you have a better understanding of what is on the mind of your prospects, return to page 31 where you wrote down the value they stand to gain by doing business with you. In the opposite column on the right, write the title "**What my prospects find valuable.**" Now write down exactly what your prospects value. This list should be independent of what you have previously written in the left-hand column (My Value).

Once you have completed this exercise, take a moment to review what you have previously written on the left side (My Value) and match it up as best as you can with what you just wrote on the right side (what your prospects find valuable).

Remember, from your prospects' point of view, most sales reps are the same — they have one thing in mind, and that's to sell them something whether they need it or not. Employing Prospect Empathy in your dialogue by aligning your specific and unique value with what your prospect finds valuable clearly differentiates you from the rest.

Now let's put it to use!

Prospect Empathy Applied

Just as a sharp axe would have saved our lumberjack friend in Chapter One a great deal of time and would have helped him reach his goal, the same can be said of our prospecting and appointment-setting skills. Having the ability to make contact with, quickly qualify, and finally convince a prospect to see you is one of the most valuable assets you could ever possess as a sales professional — and one for which companies large and small will pay big bucks.

However, these assets must be intentionally cultivated. Merely picking up the phone or walking up to a receptionist and just "winging it" is a waste of time, money and opportunity. Could you ever imagine Tiger Woods just winging it? I can see it now: there's Tiger grabbing any old club from his bag, casually walking up to the ball and taking a swing in the general direction of the green. This may be common for those of us who play golf simply for the enjoyment of being outside with friends, but this approach is unlikely for a professional like Tiger Woods. For the professional, each shot counts.

Prospecting done right builds both your financial wealth as well as your positive professional reputation. For your sake and for the sake of your prospects, take time to make sure you do things right. Make sure your value is communicated clearly, powerfully, confidently and with Prospect Empathy each and every time.

To ensure that you do just that, we have developed a process that leverages what you have learned about Prospect Empathy and helps you construct dialogue that will differentiate you from all the other sales representatives clamoring for your prospects' time, attention and business. Yes, there is a system that, when used properly, can get you the kind of results that will make your management and your banker proud.

In the next five chapters we will cover how, in a matter of a few moments, you can prepare a compelling message that, when delivered either in person, live on the telephone or through a voice-mail message, will capture attention, filter out unqualified prospects and secure appointments with those who best represent the greatest opportunities for what you offer.

Effective dialogue has **five** specific elements. Over the years we have developed **STEER,** a dialogue-enhancing technique that ensures each element is addressed, understood and acted upon with confidence. These five essential elements are:

1. **S**et the prospect at ease.
2. **T**ake control and guide the conversation.
3. **E**mpathetically illuminate your specific and unique value and gain permission to qualify.
4. **E**xpect then manage common Appointment Pushback.
5. **R**eaffirm after first confirming the appointment date, time and location.

Each essential element, when used in order, creates a dialogue that sounds natural, filters out unqualified prospects and generates enough interest in qualified prospects to keep the sales process moving. More importantly, scripts developed with STEER will differentiate you at "Hello" from all other calls experienced by your prospect! It is how your prospect perceives you from the moment of contact that spells either success or failure.

Opportunity is missed
by most people because it is dressed
in overalls and looks like work.

— THOMAS EDISON

4

STEER Element 1: Set the Prospect at Ease

SPEAKING TO A SALES REPRESENTATIVE, either on the phone or in person, can be an uncomfortable experience for some prospects. An important element of Prospect Empathy is never losing touch with what it feels like to be a prospect yourself. Prospect Empathy suggests that one of a prospects' first assumptions may be that a sales rep is calling to sell them something they already have, do not need or cannot afford. This creates a sense of defensiveness in your prospects before they ever hear your message. For your prospects to be open to your value, it is essential that they first be set at ease.

The best way to set prospects at ease is to greet them with statements of familiarity (credibility). These statements must be made early to capture your prospects' attention and interest. A powerful statement of familiarity will give you permission to speak for the next few seconds. Prospects are more at ease when they have something in common with the caller, either personally or professionally.

It is important that the statements of familiarity be communicated correctly without delay. In some cases, when your company is well-known to the prospect, your company name may provide enough familiarity and value to capture your prospect's interest and keep things moving forward. But perhaps your company is new to the area or to the industry. In this case you will need to introduce your company and its value more powerfully.

Here is an example where the caller's company name may not be known to the prospect. See how many statements of familiarity you can identify.

Assume you are calling on the manager of information technology at a local university:

"Hello, John Smith? Mike Spencer calling with Arnold Gregory & Associates — We are the IT consulting group that installed the CRM system for Second Niagara Credit Union . . ."

Did you catch all three statements of familiarity? The first is the prospect's full name pronounced correctly. The second is the CRM (Customer Relationship Management) system, a type of information system that, in his position, he would be familiar with. The third is a well-known business in his area that does business with Arnold Gregory. In less than five seconds, John Smith knows the sales rep's name, his company name, and the type of products and services his company offers. He also knows Second Niagara Credit has chosen them to implement their CRM system. At this point Mr. Smith is less defensive. In addition, when saying the prospect's full name, our inflection was in the form of a question rather than a statement of fact. This technique begins the process of engaging customers, as they will most likely follow by saying something like "Yes, what can I do for you?" You can see how we have met the objective of keeping our prospect open to listen for the next few seconds.

Compare the previous example to this common script:

"Hello, Mr. Smith, my name is Mike Spencer. I represent Arnold Gregory & Associates — How are you today?" CLICK — Mr. Smith? Hello, Mr. Smith — are you there?

Actually, Mr. Smith left the building shortly after hello. The dialogue in this example is a common approach used by many an unskilled prospector. Rather than set a prospect at ease, this dialogue actually raises suspicion. Do we really believe Mr. Smith feels that we are sincere in asking him, "How are you today?", or will he most likely just lump us in the "Oh brother, another sales call" pile, as he has heard that opening a thousand times. Even if Mr. Smith did not hang up, his perspective has most likely shifted from being neutral to the caller's message to wanting to end the call quickly.

Interestingly enough, the caller represents the same company, offers the same high-quality products and services, and has the same positive reputation with his clients. However, because the prospect was not put at ease, the caller is not allowed to communicate value, create interest and begin building the foundation of a mutually beneficial business relationship.

In this example, the caller made three big mistakes immediately. Can you pick them out?

Mistake #1: Poor Introduction
A wise man once said that the sweetest sound to anyone is the sound of his or her own name. Assuming your prospects are

decision-makers, they are called Mr., Ms. or Mrs. quite often. Once prospects hear "Mr. Smith" or whatever their last name is, they automatically assume that they are speaking with someone they do not know and have no relationship with, and who most likely wants to sell them something. Defenses go up, and your prospects become uneasy. Always address your prospects with their first and last name when making your first contact. You will clearly get their positive attention and immediately differentiate yourself from countless others who call. Take the time to say the first and last name, phrased as a question, as the next two words following "Hello," and your prospects will sit up and pay attention.

After your first face-to-face meeting, your name, company and voice will be familiar to the prospect. Your call then will be received positively, and your tone need not be as formal.

It is also important that you pronounce your prospect's name properly. Take special care to either ask a receptionist, administrative assistant or co-worker to help with pronunciation. Here is a technique used to engage the gatekeeper as your partner:

"James Tasker calling, I will be speaking with Paul later this afternoon, can you help me with the correct pronunciation of his last name?"

If you find yourself speaking directly to your prospect without the confidence of properly pronouncing his or her name, begin your call like this:

"James Tasker calling from Arnold Gregory & Associates — I must apologize, I am having trouble correctly pronouncing your name — can you help me?"

In all our years of prospecting, we have never gotten a negative response from this inquiry. Moreover, your prospects will be glad to help and will appreciate your attempt to address them properly.

Mistake #2: Useless Words
It is important to leave out useless or unnecessary words. Introducing yourself by saying "My name is" and identifying the company you are with by saying "I represent such-and-such company," adds up to about five unnecessary words. Leaving out common, useless phrases gets the same message across more effectively with fewer words.

Mistake #3: Insincere Dialogue
If ever a prospect has a red flag, it is to be asked, "How are you today?" by someone they don't know. This phrase may appear to be a courteous attempt to set a warm tone for the call. In fact, we believe the opposite occurs. The people you are speaking to understand that you are calling to determine if they are qualified prospects for your products or services. They in turn are interviewing you to discern if you have something of value for them. Getting down to business is not rude; in fact, getting to the point immediately communicates respect for their time and yours as well. We are not suggesting that your calls should take on an impersonal tone, but rather demonstrate a focused, courteous business pace.

Setting your prospect at ease is the first critical step to differentiating yourself and your company from the countless others seeking your prospect's time. A prospect at ease is more apt to "hear" to your value rather than just look for an opening to end the exchange. A prospect at ease is more likely to be open to hearing more of what you will say next. It only takes a few moments to prepare empathetic dialogue that differentiates your approach from the rest.

In the next chapter we will look at how to make the most of the next few seconds you have earned with your prospect, so as to guide the conversation to the unique value you offer.

But first, go back to your First Few Seconds Exercise on page 13 and ask yourself, "Do I set my prospects as ease or on edge? Do my prospects tune me out shortly after I say hello? Do I sound like every other sales rep?" What would you change based on what you have just learned?

In the space provided, rewrite the beginning of your approach, taking into account what you know now about setting your prospect at ease.

_____

_____

_____

_____

_____

_____

_____

_____

_____

_____

_____

_____

_____

_____

_____

_____

_____

_____

_____

_____

_____

_____

Drive thy business
or it will drive thee.

— BENJAMIN FRANKLIN

5

STEER Element 2:
Take Control and Guide the Conversation

PROSPECTING CALLS ARE MADE WITH A SPECIFIC PURPOSE in mind: to set an appointment with a qualified prospect. That said, your mission is to control the content and flow of the call. From the moment you utter your first word, your prospects are weighing the value of what you are saying against other activities they could be focusing on. In their minds, your prospects are asking themselves, *Who is this? What do they want?* and *How long will this take?* We recommend that these questions be answered quickly so that you gain control of the conversation and guide it to the next step.

Our mission is to establish a posture as a professional with something of value to share in a manner that the prospect will actually hear and not tune out like common background noise.. All the while, we must demonstrate respect for prospects' time, gratitude for the opportunity to speak with them, and assurance that we will not waste their time.

Example:

"John, thank you for taking my call — I promise to be brief."

In our example, the first word is, once again, the sweetest sound to our prospect: his first name. Within the first few seconds of your call, John has heard his name twice, leaving no doubt that this call is different from the typical sales call he has grown numb to. The prospect should be thinking, *This call might be worth listening to* (at least for the next few seconds, anyway). It is OK at this point to use the first name only.

Immediately following his name, John hears two more pleasing words: "***Thank you.***" It's sad but true: Most of us go all day, all week or even longer without hearing another human being give thanks for something we have done. Thanking your prospects for the gift of their time may be the first time they have been thanked for anything in a while. Saying "***Thank you for taking my call***" shows that we understand that their time is valuable and further separates us from other sales representatives.

"***I promise to be brief***" acknowledges that you are aware that the prospect's work day can be hectic and that your call will take up very little of their time. You can communicate that your call will be brief in a number of ways. For example, saying "I promise to be brief" is a more formal approach, working well with executive-level prospects. "I only need a moment" communicates the same message in a less formal way, and "I just need a second" is less formal still.

The prospect has no idea of the value being offered. Prospect Empathy tells us that, absent direct value to them, our prospects, if given a choice, will want to end the call quickly. From their point of view, no time is a good time to be interrupted by an unscheduled call. However, we intend to communicate something of value that is worth at least the next few seconds of their time.

Assuming you have followed STEER to this point, you have earned the right to speak for the next few seconds. In the next chapter we will explore how to deliver a powerful and compelling message that raises interest and provides your prospect with valuable reasons to allow the call to continue.

Go back and review your First Few Seconds Exercise on page 13. Are there any changes that you would make? Do the next few words out of your mouth maintain your prospect's interest and establish your control of the call? If not, in the space provided write down what you would say. Read it to yourself aloud. Then go back to your First Few Seconds Exercise and add this new dialogue. Once again, read aloud the changes you have made to this point. Sounds different, doesn't it? You are now beginning to differentiate yourself from the pack! Let's continue.

_____

_____

_____

_____

_____

_____

_____

_____

_____

_____

I never think of my audience as customers.
I think of them as partners.

— JIMMY STEWART

6

STEER Element 3:
Empathetically Illuminate Your Specific and Unique Value and Gain Permission to Qualify

As a sales representative, you are constantly competing for your prospect's time and mind share. You must quickly demonstrate to a prospect that they will benefit from continuing to speak with you for a few more moments. To do this, it is essential that your dialogue **illuminates your specific and unique value**.

Are you communicating your value to the prospect in a way that they will **hear it**? The overriding principle here is to decrease their perception of time invested, while increasing their perception of the value they will gain from the exchange.

For example: Assume for a moment that you receive a phone call from an unfamiliar party, and you detect that he has an English accent. The conversation goes something like this:

"John Peters?"

"Yes, this is John." (Thinking to himself, *This guy isn't from the neighborhood, but he still knows my name. WOW.*)

"Simon Tappley calling of Tappley, Peterman, Krumpet and Piccadilly here in London. We are the law firm responsible for

settling Sir Francis Peters' final wishes and estate."

"Oh?" (Thinking to himself, *Estate, what estate? Estates usually mean money ... Hmmm!*)

"John, I hope I have not reached you at an inconvenient time; I promise to be brief."

"Not at all; please continue." (Thinking to himself, *You have my full attention.*)

"Sir Peters has several heirs located in the U.S.A. that will share in the estate There is reason to believe that you might be one of them. Would you mind if I asked a few questions?"

"Fire away!" (Thinking to himself, *Oh boy, I'm going to be rich!*)

Notice that in this hypothetical situation, the caller held specific value that was communicated in a way that held the interest of the person being called. The caller set the prospect at ease by immediately saying his name, courteously expressing that the call would be brief and stating that the specific purpose was to see if Mr. Peters was in line to inherit a sum of money. The point here is that specific words were used to "**illuminate**" the potential value that could come from the call.

However, this call could have gone much differently:

"Mr. Preters...my name is Simon Tappley. I represent Tappley, Peterman, Krumpet and Piccadilly law firm. How are you today?"

"I'm OK." (Thinking to himself, *What is he selling that I don't need? Who is this guy, and why does he want to know how I am doing? What is so hard about pronouncing Peters?*)

"Super, I would like to ask you some questions."

Click. (Thinking to himself, *I don't have time for a survey!*)

"Mr. Preters? Are you still there? Hello? Hello?"

An extreme case, maybe, but you may recall approaches by a sales representative where the dialogue has not been far off this example. Let's see if we can do a better job maintaining our prospects' interest by "**illuminating**" our unique value.

- Once again you will find it valuable to refer to page 31, where you matched up your value with what your prospects find valuable. Review this form for a moment, as we are now going to leverage these points to the max! Our objective is to create from these benefits **Power Value Statements** to be used to generate enthusiastic interest. Here is where you must build in a prospects' mind compelling reasons why they should take time to meet with you.

Power Value Statements and the "So What?" Test

In as few words as possible, you must illuminate your unique value in language that your prospect will hear and pay attention to. Power Value Statements should generate interest and make clear to prospects that they have much to gain by listening for a few more moments. It is also very important that your Power Value

Statements pass the **"So what?"** test.

Assume for a moment that John is a new sales representative for Arnold Gregory and Associates who has completed both Value Exercises and has aligned his company's value with what his prospects find valuable.

My Value	What My Prospects Find Valuable
Best in Technology	Meeting Deadlines
Stay within Budget	Project Management Skills
On going support	Project Costs
Deliver on Time	Technical Competency
Great Reputation	Stability
	Customer Service

It looks like Arnold Gregory has a great reputation of delivering complex technical projects on time, under budget. By aligning these values with what a prospect finds valuable, our sales rep needs only to communicate the good news to the prospect. Let's see how well he does.

Example
"Arnold Gregory and Associates work with complex CRM systems. We are really good at meeting deadlines and take care not to overrun budgets."

Can you hear the prospect saying, **"So what?"** We can. Doesn't everyone say that they can handle the job, deliver on time for less money? Do you think the prospect has "heard" this before? We know they have. In fact they have heard it a lot. Perhaps they've heard it from you? If so, your message has fallen on deaf ears as your prospect has said to themselves, "**So what, so what, so what.**"

Notice how the caller communicated that Arnold Gregory & Associates are specialists, stay within budget and meet deadlines. These are strong of values, but **not** Power Value Statements in and of themselves. The sad truth is, the sales rep sounded like so many others who have called before. Thus his value was not heard by the prospect.

Let's see how a little refinement and the inclusion of Power Value Statements can make all the difference.

Example:
"Arnold Gregory and Associates specializes in design, integration and implementation of enterprise wide CRM systems. We completed our latest project at Second Niagara three weeks early and about $50,000 under budget. We'd like to be of service to Big Bucks University. Would you mind if I ask you a few questions?"

In this example, there are several **Power Value Statements**. They are as follows:

- "Specializes in enterprise wide CRM systems" (we are specialists).
- "We just completed our project at Second Niagara three weeks early" (we actually deliver on time).

- "And about $50,000 under budget" (we take care not to run projects over budget).

What the caller heard is that Arnold Gregory and Associates are specialists who complete complex projects on time and under budget. In short, this company may be of value to Big Bucks U. Because these statements pass the **"So What?"** test, perhaps now the prospect is more open and will listen for another minute.

The difference between the first example and the second is that the second example aligned the value that Arnold Gregory offers and illuminated this value by using dialogue describing a specific, quantitative example with a well-known, respected business in the industry or geographic area. Being specific maintains attention and further differentiates you from the rest.

Your task is to **identify** and **align** the value you offer with what your prospect finds valuable, then develop dialogue that **illuminates** this value in language that your prospect will "hear."

Once you develop your Power Value Statements, read them to yourself aloud. Then ask yourself, "So what?" For example, if one of your compelling reasons for a prospect to speak to you is your excellent service, ask yourself, "Has my competitor communicated that as well? Will my prospect say to themselves, 'So what?'" If so, your Power Value Statements must be enhanced with specific if not quantitative examples, reflecting successes that directly relate to what your prospects find valuable. When appropriate, these examples can be empowered when the satisfied client is a well known or respected business in the prospect's geographical area or industry.

If your company is a new start up and or has little or no track record to draw from, then the Power Value Statements may be based on or founded in your stated commitment to excellence, or a specific guarantee to customer satisfaction.

Gain Permission to Qualify

At this stage in the dialogue, prospects must begin to feel that they have something valuable to gain or that they may have something valuable to lose if they don't take the time to speak with you. At the same time, you are assessing the prospect's value to you and your company as well. Are you speaking with the right person, and is the person qualified for your offering?

Take a moment and picture your ideal prospects. What is it about them or their current state that makes them a candidate for your offering? Are they at the end of a long-term lease with your competitor? Are they expanding their operations? Are they contracting or consolidating? What is the level of opportunity?

Well-constructed qualifying questions will help your prospects identify themselves as prime candidates for more of your time, or they will disqualify themselves, freeing you to move on. Also, if done right, qualifying questions should actually begin selling the value of your product and of doing business with you. For this reason, we consider qualifying questions to be very important to your success. They warrant an investment on your part to develop them. For example, in the printing industry, here's one incorrect qualifying question that is often asked:

"What is your monthly print volume, or more specifically, how many pages per month do you produce in your operation?"

This question just asks for a number. Based on the number (if known off the top of the prospect's head), your typical sales rep may either qualify or disqualify the prospect. However, the prospect feels like having answered a survey without a specific purpose. What about the prospect's business objectives? Will the answer to the question do anything to bring value to the prospect? Where is the Prospect Empathy here?

On the other hand, words can paint pictures. Observe the following technique for asking a volume-type question in a "prospect empathetic" fashion:

"Is your current equipment able to maintain the print quality your customers demand during peak production periods?"

There are only three answers to this qualifying question:

1. Yes, everything is just fine (we have no problem).
2. No, I cannot keep up with the demand (my problem is I need more capacity).
3. Yes, but my equipment is underutilized (I need more print volume to be profitable).

This qualifying question asks more than just how much volume is run. The prospect is now thinking not only about his print volume, but also about whether his customers are truly happy with the quality and turnaround the company provides. We are looking for problems or issues that our offering can address to our prospect's advantage.

We recommend you construct your qualifying questions in such a way that your prospects take a closer look at their current state of affairs as being either positive or negative. Qualifying questions cause prospects to think in such a way that it builds their desire to involve you in making a change for the better.

You need to determine what traits or characteristics make up the ideal prospect. For some, any warm body over age 18 with a checkbook will do. For others, qualified prospects meet criteria of authority, budget, geography, environment issues and so on. One thing is certain: A truly qualified prospect is one who is either already motivated to make a change or can be motivated to do so.

It is vital that you construct your questions so as to uncover specific characteristics about your prospects, as well as to get them thinking about how wonderful and painless it would be to make a change. Consider the following about the people you are speaking with, their company and the state of change within it, their satisfaction with their current vendor, and their openness to considering alternatives:

- Is the person you are speaking with the decision-maker or major influencer?
- Can this person use (if not already using) a product or service that you provide?
- Are there any barriers to doing business with you?
- How would your product or service effect positive change?

You will find that your best prospecting calls turn into miniature business discussions rather than surveys or interviews. After asking your qualifying questions and receiving answers, you can now discern whether there is a compelling reason to meet with your prospect for a more formal sales call (or appointment). As your prospects have been heavily involved in your conversation, they may have already concluded that it is worth their time as well. By following STEER, you are in control of the call; it is up to you to set the appointment.

Gaining a time commitment from your prospect can be a bit tricky, depending upon schedules and level of interest. Remember, your prospect is most likely quite busy, and adding one more activity to their schedule is generally not on the top of their to-do list. It is imperative that scheduling a meeting with you is as convenient and trouble-free for your prospect as possible.

Many sales trainers and successful reps use a technique that offers the prospect a choice of days and times. Here's an example:

"Would Tuesday at 1:00 work for you, or is Thursday at 4:00 better?"

We have heard this technique used and taught for years. Many successful sales representatives use this technique and get good results. However, we have both had conversations that go something like this:

Rep: *"Would Tuesday at 1:00 work for you, or is Thursday at 4:00 better?"*

Prospect: *"Let's see, Tuesday at 1:00 won't work and Thursday afternoon is our staff meeting."*

Rep: *"OK, how about Tuesday at 3:00 or maybe Thursday at 10:00"?*

Prospect: *"Tuesday afternoon I have a demonstration off site, and Thursday morning is my dentist appointment."*

You get the picture. Although effective in some cases, this technique can result in the rep chasing prospects around their calendars. The longer they do this, the more likely they will talk themselves out of the potential value.

We suggest you say something like the following:

"John, the rest of this week is crazy for me as I imagine it may be for you. What days next week do you already have completely scheduled?"

We have found that asking our prospects to assess when they are not available enhances their ability to identify and acknowledge openings in their schedule. Unless they are out of town or on vacation during that week, they will recognize their availability and be able to tell you immediately.

Also notice that we expressed to the prospect that we are busy as well by communicating that our first availability for an appointment will be the following week. Asking for the appointment for the following week often reduces prospects' "time anxiety," as well as adds to their perception that your time is also of value.

Getting prospects to admit to and identify available time on their coveted calendars is not the only obstacle to overcome in becoming an Appointment Machine. In the next chapter we will address what we call **Appointment Pushback** — why it should be expected and welcomed, and how to successfully manage it.

But first, go back to your First Few Seconds Exercise on page 13 and ask yourself if your unique value is "aligned" with what your prospects find valuable and is communicated in a way that your prospects will hear. Are your words "illuminating" your value? If not, take a few moments and practice in the space provided.

_____

_____

_____

_____

_____

_____

_____

_____

_____

_____

_____

_____

_____

_____

_____

_____

_____

_____

_____

_____

_____

_____

_____

_____

_____

_____

Go confidently in the direction
of your dreams.
Live the life you have imagined.

— HENRY DAVID THOREAU

7

STEER Element 4:
Expect Then Manage Appointment Pushback

MOST OF US HAVE BECOME SKILLED at avoiding additional time commitments. Understanding this, it is easy to see why there can be some initial resistance from prospects when it comes to committing to an appointment with you or anyone else. Resistance to granting an appointment is normal and can actually help you better understand your prospects, as well as help you more effectively spend your time with only the prospects qualified for your offering.

Notice that this element is titled "Expect Then *Manage Appointment Pushback*," not "Expect Then Handle Objections." "*Handling objections*" implies that all you need to do to convince your prospects to spend time with you is answer every one of their concerns. The fact is, though, that some objections simply cannot be overcome. There are people you simply do not want to take your time to meet with. For example, "I am just not interested" is an objection that is tough to overcome consistently.

Your objective is to meet only with prospects open to seeing you and exploring your offering. Those who are not interested are simply not a good investment of your time.

Timing is also important. Through your prospecting efforts, you will undoubtedly come across those who are qualified for your offering but cannot act, or will not set an appointment because the timing is not right. Perhaps they are in the middle of a long-term contract with one of your competitors, or perhaps your prospects are new to their positions and not yet ready to evaluate new vendors. Becoming skilled at **Managing Appointment Pushback** will help you further sift through your prospects, identify those who are indeed qualified, eliminate those who are not, and keep you in touch with those who are prime candidates for your offering in the future.

Out of instinct alone, even qualified prospects may push back at your request for an appointment — it's almost a natural reaction. Understanding this can help you reveal a qualified prospect whose hesitation is a knee-jerk reaction, as compared to the reaction of an unqualified prospect.

With few exceptions, it wouldn't be productive if every time you called prospects they enthusiastically pulled out their calendars and penciled you in, or if they said, "I'd love to make time for you; just say when and where." If you could sit down with everyone you called, you may find out after a 30-minute appointment that some are not qualified for your offering. With that in mind, look at a prospect's hesitation as an opportunity to gather more information for better managing your calendar.

Appointment Pushback tells you a great deal about your prospects, their situations and how open they are to doing business with you. Don't miss this great opportunity to continue to sell the value of a relationship with you and your company.

Appointment Pushback also tells you how effective, or "empathetic" your Power Value Statements are. Don't fear Pushback; knowing it's coming is to your advantage. You can learn how qualified your prospects really are, as well as how much time should you devote to them.

Most Pushback to an appointment is predictable and thus can be managed relatively consistently. There are really only four primary Pushbacks to an appointment. They are:

1. Status Quo
2. No Time
3. The Brush-Off
4. Tell Me More

The good news is that with only four primary forms of Pushback to deal with, it's easy to arm yourself to comfortably and confidently manage them in such a way that you can maintain control of the call and confirm appointments with only qualified prospects.

Let's look at each Pushback in more detail:

Status Quo
The Status Quo Pushback is probably the most commonly used defense against an appointment and can be employed by qualified and unqualified prospects alike. In short, your prospect tells you that they already have what you offer, believe they are happy with the way things are and are not interested in change. You will know the Pushback is a Status Quo type if you hear things like, "I'm

covered," or "Our equipment works just fine," or "We are on a long-term contract," and so on.

No Time

When experiencing the No-Time Pushback, you will often hear something like "I'm too busy" as a knee-jerk reaction from a prospect who is looking for any excuse not to commit to anything. It will sound like, "I'm booked for the next few weeks," or "This month is bad for me."

The Brush-Off

The Brush-Off Pushback is typically used by a prospect who does not consider your company to be a viable vendor. The Brush-Off goes something like this: "Can you send me some information?" or "Do you have a Web site I can take a look at?" or "Send me some literature and if I am interested, I'll get back to you." Last but not least, there is our favorite: The Psychic Brush-Off. This is when the prospect tells you that they are not interested in what you are offering before you ever have a chance to tell them what you are calling about.

Tell Me More

With the Tell Me More Pushback, the prospect says something like, "Let's just skip the appointment; tell me everything now." Usually this Pushback is given during phone prospecting. Depending upon your product or service, you may want to continue. If meeting this person face to face is important, you need to be prepared to manage this so as to successfully set up an appointment.

How Best to Manage Appointment Pushback

Clearly the best way to manage any resistance to an appointment is to address the prospect's concern up front. The time you invested developing your Power Value Statements will go a long way to eliminating much of the common Pushback. Remember, a strong Power Value Statement delivered empathetically may totally disarm your prospect's Pushback. However, as stated earlier, some prospects cannot help themselves and will push back out of habit alone.

For these prospects that naturally push back, a prepared strategy to manage common Pushback is essential. We have found that all **qualified** prospects share at least one of four common traits, if not all of them. In general (and we must for the moment speak in general terms), **qualified** prospects want to be perceived as:

1. Being well informed and knowledgeable about their area of expertise.
2. Business-savvy.
3. Courteous and likable, honest and fair.
4. Having a strongly positive business reputation.

Think about it: Would you want to do business with someone with a poor reputation, with no sense of fairness, who does not care to be informed, or who is rude and unlikable? Of course not. Spending time chasing unqualified prospects will waste your time and energy, and wear down your positive attitude.

Those who do have a good reputation, a strong sense of fairness, like to be in the know and who are generally polite, are great people to deal with and will find it easy to say yes to an appointment with someone offering something of value to share. These are the kind of people who make our jobs fun and rewarding.

However, some prospects may need to be **reminded** just how fair, well informed and courteous they really are. The stresses of everyday living and working create the kind of pressure that can sometimes make even the most amiable people appear short-tempered, aggressive and rude. Having a little empathy for your prospect can go a long way toward guiding you through even the toughest calls and to protecting your attitude and momentum. Have you ever had "one of those days"? Chances are your prospects have also. Your call may happen to come on "one of these days" for them. Don't sweat it.

Appointment Pushback is easily managed by following a few simple steps:

1. Acknowledge and Absorb the Pushback.
2. Illuminate the positive traits of a qualified prospect.
3. Eliminate appointment risk while increasing your value.
4. Evaluate your prospect's response.

Acknowledge and Absorb the Pushback
When met with a prospect's resistance, the last thing you want to do is dismiss the fact that your prospect has raised an issue or in any way respond defensively. However, acknowledging the issue tells the prospect that you recognize that, from the prospect's point of view, the concern is valid. This does not mean that you agree with the prospect. Agreeing gives unnecessary power to the Pushback. Absorbing the Pushback tells your prospect that you

are not shaken by the Pushback and do not take offense to it.

I (JT) will illustrate these simple yet powerful principles with a fictional example of a prospect commenting (negatively) on one of my favorite ties. Unbeknownst to the prospect, this tie was a gift from my 9-year-old son. The individual posing as the "fashion police" delivers a rude response to an invitation to attend a father/child home-wardrobe party.

JT: *"Fred Smith — Grant Baker calling; we met at our son's soccer game last week"* (set at ease with familiarity).

Fred: *"Oh, yes, how are you doing?"*

JT: *"I'm great, Fred; I know you are probably busy, so I'll make this brief"* (take control).

Fred: *"Not a problem. What can I do for you?"*

JT: *"Fred, I am having a father/child get-together next Tuesday evening at 7:00. It's a men's wardrobe party where children get to pick out a special tie as a Father's Day gift — we would love to have you and Max join us."*

Fred: *"That sounds interesting, but JT, I've got to tell you, I have seen you wear some of the ugliest ties I have ever seen. Is your kid colorblind?"* (Need we mention this is a rude response?)

Answering this Pushback by saying something like, "No, they aren't ugly!" or "I don't think my son is colorblind!" neither absorbs nor acknowledges Fred's rude response. At this point, it's one person's opinion against another. However, we can choose to take a different approach by saying something like:

"Oh, you must have seen the yellow goose tie" (acknowledge). "I get a lot of attention when I wear that crazy tie" (absorb).

This approach tells the prospect that he is not the only one who notices JT's unique tie and that we understand his point of view even if his expression is rude and might have caused tension under normal circumstances.

Illuminate the Positive Traits of Qualified Prospects
Your prospect may not fully understand what good will come from granting a meeting with you. Before restating the value of your offering, it is a good idea to remind your prospects that they are likable, business-savvy and fair individuals with great reputations, and therefore should be open to looking at the value your offering can bring them.

Continuing with our ugly-tie example, I say:

"Fred, I hear you are a pretty involved parent (good reputation). You know it's the little things that mean so much to children (knowledgeable/likable). Imagine the look in your little boy's eyes when he sees you go out the door wearing the tie he picked out just for you (value). You may get some comments from time to time, but a little boy's memories (value) seem worthwhile, don't you think?" (fair).

After that, do you think Fred really sees an ugly tie, or does he see a way to add joy to his son's life by attending a special event and wearing something he helped pick out?

Re-invite by Expressing the Need for a Face-to-Face Appointment With a Small Time Commitment
At this point, your prospects believe that you understand their Pushbacks, have been reminded of their positive traits, and more clearly understand the value of taking the time to see you. Now they may be more open to your request for a meeting. Illustrate how a small time investment on their part may yield significant benefits.

"We are getting together at my house Thursday evening from 7:00 to 7:30 (small time investment), and again the following Tuesday for those who can't make it Thursday. Which day do you and Kieth prefer to stop by?" (Note: This example illustrates an invitation to an event with definitive dates, times and locations. In this example, an "either/or" approach to gain commitment is acceptable and necessary.)

Evaluate Your Prospect's Response
If the prospect agrees to your second invitation, you should immediately move on to secure the appointment. If your prospect does not respond positively, respectfully end the call. You can then move on to your next prospect and be glad you saved yourself time and energy, and protected your attitude.

Let's take a closer look at some examples of how to best identify and manage common Appointment Pushback.

Status Quo
Prospects that offer a **Status Quo** Pushback:

CHAPTER SEVEN

- May or may not be happy with their current situation.
- Will expend a lot of effort to avoid change.
- Is not aware of the additional value of doing business with you.

When managing a **Status Quo** Pushback, it is acceptable to build a bit of "prospect envy" to move your prospect to the point of considering change. It is important to communicate to your prospect:

- How well-off your customers are because they do business with you (they have something the prospect does not).
- The relative ease of a transition to doing business with you.
- Any specific and unique value that a business relationship with you may bring.

All the while remind prospects just how well-informed, business-savvy and fair they are.

Here is a bad example of how to respond to the Status Quo Pushback:

Prospect: *"We use XYZ's products and are happy with them. Call back in six months and check in with us then."*

Sales Rep: *"I am sure we could save you some money. Can I stop by to show you our prices?"*

Prospect: *"No, not now, but feel free to fax me a quote if you want, or just give us a call in six months or so."*

STEER Element 4:
Expect Then Manage Appointment Pushback

Sadly, if this sales rep does not get better at managing Status Quo Pushback, he or she will not call back in six months because they will be employed elsewhere. If the rep does manage to stay around long enough to call back six months later, the business relationship has not progressed one bit. This sales rep is still just a voice on the phone.

Now this sales rep may be representing a great company that could provide significant value to the prospect. But this value will be lost because the sales rep took the approach that cost savings alone would outweigh the trouble and inconvenience associated with making a change.

Remember, *prospects who use a Status Quo Pushback to resist your request for an appointment are not saying no to you or your company; they are saying no to the process of change.*

Let's assume for a moment that the sales rep took the time to learn how to properly manage Appointment Pushback. Note the Pushback management techniques:

Prospect: *"We use XYZ's products and seem to be happy. Call back in six months and check in with us then."*

Sales Rep: *"XYZ is a fine company; I compete with them all the time. What I often find is that customers who switch to us enjoy our more flexible delivery schedule and online order tracking — in fact, we customized PB&J's delivery schedule to fit their manufacturing peaks. This actually helped win a rather large contract for PB&J. My contact Ed is a big hero now.*

"Getting together for a few moments will help me learn more about your operation so I can do a better job for you when the time comes.

"I don't know if we could do the same for you as we did for PB&J, but it would only take about 20 minutes to find out — besides, It would be great to exchange business cards — does that sound fair?"

In this example, the prospect is given the opportunity to demonstrate their business savvy by taking just a little time to learn about what the sales rep's company did for PB&J. Besides, they are courteous, likable and fair, so exchanging business cards seems easy enough.

If the prospect still does not agree to meet, it is important to gain their permission to stay in touch. Periodically putting your name, your company and your product in front of your prospect all but ensures that you will be given consideration when the time comes. The only sure thing is that change is ever-present and will continue to affect your prospects and customers over time. Staying in touch ensures you have the opportunity to prosper from change.

No Time
Prospects who offer a **No Time** Pushback most likely:

- Believe their time is better spent working on projects unrelated to your offering.
- Do not want to start a project that will put one more thing on their plate.

- Would make time for you if there were a compelling value that would somehow make their business life easier, or in some way make them look good.

When managing the **No Time** pushback, it is important to communicate to your prospects:

- How little time it really will take to consider your offering.
- An understanding that meeting with you does not necessarily mean a new project will fall in their lap.
- A potentially big payoff that requires a small time investment on their part.

All the while remind them just how well-informed, business-savvy and fair they are.

The Brush-Off

A prospect that tries The **Brush-Off** most likely:

- Does not perceive your company as a viable supplier.
- May not be appropriate for you to call on.

When managing a **Brush-Off** pushback, it is important to communicate to your prospects that:

- Your company is a viable vendor with unique value.
- It will be great for them to be the one who discovered you.
- If they are not the proper contact, their company stands to gain value by passing you on to the proper contact.

All the while remind them just how well-informed, business-savvy and fair they are.

Action Item
You will notice there are script-building forms in the back of the book. Use these forms to write down at least three of the most common Pushbacks you may get in each of the three categories on the left side. Now take the time to write down your responses for each, taking into account what you have just read. Remember, most Pushbacks to an appointment will fall into one of these four categories:

- Status Quo
- No Time
- The Brush-Off
- Tell Me More

Have this form available when you construct your custom scripts so that you will better manage each type of Appointment Pushback as they come up.

But What Do I Do if They Say Something I Haven't Thought of? This is a good question. It is possible that you may get a Pushback that you feel does not fall into any one of the categories. Typically your prospect has asked a specific question that will require some research. It would be great to have something to say that acknowledges your prospect's question and keeps you in control of the call. When confronted with Pushback we have not heard before, we use something like this:

Prospect: *[Asks a question you have not yet heard.]*

Rep: *"Good question. This is the first time I've been asked that. Let me do some research and I'll have an answer for you when we get together"* (assume the appointment and move on to confirm it).

In this example, we don't shy away from the question or let the prospect think in any way that we do not want to answer it. Simply acknowledge that the question is a good one, that you simply don't have an answer at the moment, but that it is important to you that you get an answer by the time of the appointment.

Now that we've equipped you to expect, and then successfully manage, the inevitable Appointment Pushback, let's help you finish the STEER process by confirming and reaffirming the date, time and place of the appointment.

Diligence is the
Mother of good luck.

— BENJAMIN FRANKLIN

8

STEER Element 5: Reaffirm After Confirming

IT WOULD BE A CALAMITY if either you or your prospect made a mistake about the time or place of a scheduled appointment. Confirming, and in all cases reaffirming, your appointments is well worth the effort and will save you a lot of time.

When you set your appointment, the following dialogue works well for every prospect type. Here is an example of what we use — date, time and location are the keys:

(Prospect agrees to meet)

Rep: *"OK, that's 10:00 Tuesday the 5th in your office at 34 South University Avenue"* [confirm].

Prospect: *"Yes, that's right."*

Rep: *"Great, I am writing in my calendar 10:00 next Tuesday at your office on South University"* [reaffirm].

Prospect: *"See you then."*

In this example, the prospect has heard the day and/or date (Tuesday the 5th) twice, the time (10:00) twice, and the location (his office on South University) twice as well. Without being redundant, we have reaffirmed each critical schedule component.

We find that saying, "I am writing in my calendar... " draws prospects' attention to the day and time on their calendar as well. They know that you will be there and that it is written in stone.

STEER In Review

1. **S**et the prospect at ease.
2. **T**ake control and guide the conversation.
3. **E**mpathetically illuminate your specific and unique value and gain permission to qualify.
4. **E**xpect then manage common Appointment Pushback.
5. **R**eaffirm after first confirming the appointment date, time and location.

Each essential element, when used in order, creates a dialogue that sounds natural, filters out unqualified prospects and generates enough interest from qualified prospects to keep the sales process moving.

(This page intentionally left blank.)

Well done is better than *Well said*.

— BENJAMIN FRANKLIN

9

Build Referrals with STEER

OH, THE POWER OF THE REFERRAL.

One plus one equals five. New math? No, referral math. Every prospect is a referral source who can lead you to another prospect, who is a referral source who can lead you to another prospect who is a referral... Well, you get the idea.

There is no doubt that referrals can mean big money to the professional sales representative. However, asking for referrals is an often-neglected practice, and if not neglected, it is frequently rendered ineffective by poor referral-generating techniques.

If you have been a sales professional for any period of time, you have most likely heard it suggested that all you need to do to get referrals is **just ask!** For example, saying something to your prospects like, "Can you do me a favor — who do you know that may be a good candidate for what I am offering?"

Perhaps you have asked a prospect or current customer for this favor and have ended up empty-handed. After a few failed attempts, you may have thought to yourself that perhaps this asking-for-referrals thing isn't such a good idea after all. If any of this sounds familiar, you will find the next few pages extremely valuable.

It's All About Benefit to the Customer or Prospect

The first lesson in building a large referral base is to have a long-term vision of the referral process, rather than the all-too-common, short-sighted "Give me some names so I can move on" approach.

The truth is that **referrals are earned**. To increase the probability of prospects or clients enthusiastically supplying you with quality referrals, it is essential that you first demonstrate your value in such a way that the referring prospects or clients view the act of giving the referral as being more of a favor to the people they are referring you to, than a favor to you. The prospect or client who believes that they are giving you a referral, more so as a favor to the people they are referring you to, is more apt to furnish you with quality referrals throughout your business relationship.

OK, you may be saying, "I get the point. I must earn the referral by creating a level of value to where the referral given is perceived as less a favor to me than it is to the person I will be calling. That much I understand. But when do I ask for the referral? I do still have to ask for the referral, don't I?" Good question, and here is the best answer we can give: It depends!

Not only knowing how to, but also just as important, when to ask for referrals, is key to increasing the probability that you will succeed in adding quality prospects to your list. There are those times when you can earn the referral on your initial call. Other times it may take months or even years before it is appropriate and/or fruitful to ask for a referral and expect it to be freely and or enthusiastically given. This is the second, and oftentimes over looked, lesson in building a large base of professional referrals.

Remember, when prospects give referrals, they have put their personal stamp of approval on you and the value you will bring to their personal or professional acquaintances. Therefore, it is understandable why some people may hesitate and why it is always your responsibility to first develop a level of trust and confidence in you, your company and the value you bring to that referral.

How Referrals Are Earned

It is imperative that you treat every prospect and existing client as if each one represents 100 referrals; they just may. Always presenting yourself in a professional manner can pay long-term dividends. When prospecting, treat people in a way that leaves them comfortable with you and your company. If they are comfortable with you, they are more apt to believe that you will treat their professional acquaintances with the same level of courtesy and respect. Remember, your goal is to present yourself in such a way that those who give you the name of a referral will do so with the confidence that the people they have referred you to will thank them for sending you their way.

Earning referrals depends on three things:
1. Following STEER when making your initial contact.
2. Providing value to prospects even if they do not buy from you today, tomorrow or ever.
3. Keeping in touch.

Let's look at each of these topics in a bit more detail.

Following STEER should need little explanation by now. STEER all but ensures that you, your company and your value are differentiated from your competition. Your prospect sees and hears you differently, thus is more apt to allow a relationship to develop over time. STEER establishes the framework for you to become "well known" to your prospect. Being well known further instills comfort and builds trust. You can bet that prospects will hesitate to share information with you if they do not comfortably trust you.

Providing Value means that you establish yourself as a valuable resource. This can be as simple as passing on a lead for new business to your prospect or customer. Remember, your prospects have interests of their own, both professional and personal. It takes little effort to "keep an eye out" for something that your prospect will find valuable. Perhaps you occasionally pass on a lead for new business to your prospect, or mail a handwritten note along with a photocopy of a newspaper article that your prospect may find of interest. It is important that your efforts to provide service and add value are genuine, with no strings attached. You know you are providing value when your prospects or customers periodically call you to ask your opinion on your particular area of expertise.

Keeping in Touch on a regular basis is just good business. Consistent contact over time gives your prospect the assurance that you value the relationship. A phone call, a voice mail, an e-mail or a formal keep-in-touch program keeps you in the game.

You may be asking yourself, "How do I tactfully ask a prospect or customer for a referral, and what do I say when I approach the person I've been referred to?" Great question. Here are some suggestions and sample dialogue.

Asking for the Referral

Now that you are armed with the awareness and confidence of the unique and specific value you offer, it is essential that your dialogue illuminates this value for your prospect or the one to whom you are being referred. For example, saying something like "Who do you know that I might call on?" implies that you are interested in their established contacts and/or relationships solely for your benefit. However, by saying something like **"Who do you know that I may help or be of service to?"** softens the approach and illuminates your intent to serve and benefit the referral. It is important to ask the people who refer prospects to you to identify their relationship with the referrals so you can refer to these by name. Once you receive the referral, applying STEER to the approach all but ensures the referral won't be wasted.

Using STEER to Contact a Referral

Contacting a referral is slightly different that contacting someone with whom you have no association. In fact, it is much easier, since the referral can be more readily set at ease by referencing the association you both share with the person who referred you. In the following example, the sales rep had asked for and received a referral from a satisfied customer. See if you can identify all the STEER elements in the dialogue.

Rep: *"Hello, Don Spencer? Frank Miller calling with Industrial Supply Co. — We have a common acquaintance in Robert Hall."*

CHAPTER NINE

Don: *"Hello, Frank Miller. How is our good friend Robert?"*

Rep: *"Great, he says hello — Don; do you have just a few moments?"*

Don: *"I have a few moments. How can I help you?"*

Rep: *"Don, my company specializes in saving mid-to-large printing plants up to 50% on industrial cleaning supplies while exceeding the latest EPA standards — I'd like to sit down with you for 20 minutes or so and explore if we could be of service to you — what days next week are you completely tied up?"*

Don: *"I think we are all set for now. We get our supplies from Universal Supply Co. We've been with them for years, but thank you for calling."*

Rep: *"I see. I am familiar with them and actually compete with them often. My customers find our prices and timely delivery to be a significant benefit. I'm not sure how much money we may be able to save you, but it would take only a few moments to find out. When we sit down, I can put together a few numbers. If it looks like we can serve you better, then perhaps there is good reason to get together again. If not, nothing lost. Does that sound fair to you?"*

Don: *"Yes, that sounds fair, but I must tell you that I am not a real good prospect. My brother-in-law is my rep from Universal Supply. If I make a change, I would most likely be spending time in divorce court."*

Rep: *"Thank you so much for letting me know. I guess it would not be a convenient time for us to do business. If you don't mind, I'd like to check in from time to time. Perhaps someday your brother-in-law may move on to a different company and we could get together then."*

Here, the rep was dealing with an unqualified prospect from the start. Nothing the rep could have said would have changed that. Don's relationship with his current supplier made it impossible for him to do business with anyone else, so an appointment would have been a waste of time.

Further, even though the request for an appointment was rejected, the rep came out just fine. He wasn't rejected personally; there simply was no business opportunity at that specific time.

One Last Question
Before hanging up, the rep did not overlook the opportunity to ask one last question:

Rep: *"Don, one last question — if you were me, who would you call in the area that I may be able to help?"*

Don: *"If I were you, I'd call Remley's on Harvest Drive; they might be a good prospect for you."*

Rep: *"Thanks again. Who should I ask for when I call Remley's?"*

Don: *"Ask for Jim Remley. He is a good friend of mine. You can tell him we spoke. Tell him I suggested you call."*

Rep: *"Don, you have been a great help; thank you again. I'll stay in touch."*

There are several points to take note of in the above dialogue. First, the sales rep first had the proper mindset that says, Wha*t I offer is of value*, and had empathy and knew the need for the product. Then the rep coupled that by setting the prospect at ease through strong statements of familiarity. As a result, the prospect was put at ease and made comfortable with the call, thus was more than happy to pass on Jim Remley's name as a referral.

Now, when calling Jim, the rep will not sound like just another sales rep. The call has been *recommended* by Jim's good friend Don. They already have the beginnings of a relationship, and chances are high that Jim will treat the caller in the same fair and courteous manner he would treat his good friend Don.

In this example, the sales rep followed STEER to the letter and won. Why do we say the sales rep won? Well, look at the result. A contact was made with a prospect that, although not qualified at the present time, gave permission to stay in touch. A new relationship has begun. In addition, the relationship generated a referral who will most likely become a new active prospect, or at the very least will be added to the growing list of prospects who are open to having the rep stay in touch as a contender for future business. Sounds like a win to us!

(This page intentionally left blank.)

You can't build a reputation on what you are
GOING TO DO.

— HENRY FORD

10

Prepare to Prosper

Preparing Your Environment for Results

WHETHER MAKING CALLS FROM YOUR HOME or an office, it is important that you prepare your surroundings to minimize any possible distractions. We suggest that you take care to **seek privacy**. It is important that you are undisturbed while making your calls. Here are some suggestions that may help:

Take Care of Incoming Calls

The time you dedicate to prospecting is for only that — prospecting. That means you should not take any incoming calls. You are in an important meeting (with yourself) that deserves the same respect as any other. It is a good idea to forward your phone to another number that is either staffed or equipped with voice mail. Chances are good that you may call someone who cannot talk at that moment but may call you back before you have finished making your calls for the day. By having a secondary callback number or having the call-forwarding option engaged, you will avoid interruption and you won't miss an important return call.

Disable Call Waiting

The call-waiting tone can be distracting. To play it safe, we recommend disabling this feature while prospecting. You'll find the instructions for disabling call waiting in your local phone book.

Cellular Phones

The portable nature of today's cellular phones makes them a popular choice for today's business professional. We remember when they were called car phones because they were bolted to the dashboard and only worked with the engine running. Portability makes today's cellular phones a great business tool, especially when seeking privacy. However, nothing is worse than having one party be unable to hear the other. A weak cellular signal can spell disaster for prospecting calls. Therefore, we suggest that whenever possible, go land-line for these important calls.

Call Quality and Accurate Record Keeping

We recommend taking notes while prospecting, always being prepared to write down immediately all pertinent information given by your prospect during the call. This includes answers to your questions, business climate, prospect values, current and upcoming business schedule, client's business status, goals, current and future needs, competitive vendor or standing proposals, and statements of Appointment Pushback, as well as confirming information on the times and locations of your appointments successfully set.

The use of a **quality headset** — leaving both hands available — can be to your great advantage. Without the use of a quality headset, the probability of avoidable distractions is increased.

Try the following experiment with a colleague: Request that they call you using a standard handset, and during the conversation, ask that they switch the handset from one ear to the other a couple of times. The noises you hear as the phone moves from position to position can be distracting to your prospect. Or worse yet, your voice can end up sounding muffled or muted completely from the sheer act of holding the phone in place with your chin while attempting to talk and write notes at the same time. A headset eliminates these distractions. We can't emphasize enough the value of the investment in a quality headset.

Additional Tips to Fortify Call Success

You are now well aware that setting the prospect at ease is the first important step when making a successful contact. With that in mind, there are other factors you can control to best maximize the favorability of your reception. The following are simple yet powerful suggestions that will affect your success.

When Do I Call?

The answer to this question is industry-specific. If you have a coach, ask the coach about the best prospecting time for your profession or industry. If a coach is not available, here are some guidelines to start with:

When Calling A Private Residence

As a general rule, calls to a private residence become less popular for every minute that inches after 9 p.m. or before 8:30 a.m. We suggest you set your schedule to complete your calls prior to 9 p.m. The only exception is when you know for a fact that your prospect takes late-evening calls.

Similarly, calls around the dinner hour have their own issues. These issues can be handled quite well by opening with, "Did I reach you at a bad time?" This technique allows you to assess the prospect's receptiveness of your call, as well as to establish control of the conversation.

Practice Makes Permanent

Customized dialogue has been proven to generate superior results. However, even the best script can fail if not delivered properly. To take full advantage of the work put into customizing scripts, it is a good idea to practice until your words sound confident and natural.

Practicing does not mean merely reading each script over once or twice. It means first rehearsing alone, then with a tape recorder, in front of a mirror, and finally with a coach. A solid hour of practice will pay dividends for years to come.

Practice Alone in Front of a Mirror

Find a quiet place to read your script as if you are speaking to a prospect out loud. It is important that you hear your voice speak your scripts. It will help if you smile when you read your scripts. It is true that a smile can be heard. To prove this point, the next time you listen to talk radio, listen to the on-air personalities and ask yourself if you can picture their facial expressions as they speak. Based on their voice tones and inflections, can you picture in your mind's eye when they are smiling during their conversation? It is surprisingly easy to do. Your smile truly can be heard!

Practice each script until you begin to feel the words, inflections and pauses sounding natural. It is important that your scripts sound conversational, meaning that oftentimes the written word sounds odd, scripted or canned. Focus more on how your words "sound" conversationally rather than on how they read on paper. Practicing your scripts in front of a mirror can be especially beneficial if in-person prospecting is part of your appointment-setting strategy.

Practice With a Tape Recorder
A simple tape recorder can be a powerful self-training tool. A tape recorder acts as a "voice mirror," offering you a true reflection of how you will sound to your prospect. Record your voice and play back each script while imagining that you are the receiver of the call. Do you sound confident, natural and in control? If not, practice until you do. Before you know it, you will.

Practice With a Coach
Ask a good friend or mentor to role-play with you as you make practice calls to them. Ask them to assume the roles
of the types of prospects you call on most often. Be sure that they offer resistance in the form of some Pushback. Refer to your Appointment Pushback scripts to practice managing each response type. Ask for honest feedback.

But What About Gatekeepers?
Gatekeepers are those people who stand between you and your prospect. They are frequently instructed to screen incoming calls to protect the prospect's time either at home or at work. The likelihood that the gatekeeper will be the person who answers your call is quite high. You can put a gatekeeper on *high alert* if your voice is unfamiliar or if you mispronounce the prospect's name.

Your goal is to either avoid gatekeepers altogether by tactfully circumventing their screening process, or gain their approval so that they pass your call on to your prospect.

Gatekeepers fall into two main categories:

1. Corporate or company gatekeeper (administrative assistant, receptionist or subordinate, for example)
2. Domestic gatekeeper (spouse, child or baby sitter)

Corporate Gatekeepers

A time-tested technique we have successfully used to bypass corporate or company gatekeepers is to call during off-hours to catch prospects unguarded. Before 7:30 a.m., at exactly 12:15 p.m., after 5:30 p.m. or on Saturdays at 11:00 a.m. are prime times to catch prospects at their desk. It is not uncommon to find many professionals at work early, eating lunch at their desks, working after hours and occasionally coming into the office on a Saturday. Most gatekeepers work normal business hours from 8 a.m. to 5 p.m. taking either an hour or half-hour for lunch. These are prime times to call, as your prospect is now unguarded.

Placing a call directly to your prospect during unguarded times greatly increases your chances that he or she will actually pick up the phone. For this technique to work, you will need to obtain your prospect's direct-dial number. You can usually get a person's work direct-dial number simply by calling the main company switchboard and asking the receptionist. If your prospect does not answer directly, you will most likely end up in voice mail, where you can leave a message. (We discuss voice mail later in this chapter.)

Another technique to get connected directly to your prospect is to call the main switchboard and ask for accounts receivable. The people in this department know everyone in the company and will most likely not only give you your prospect's direct-dial number, but may also transfer you directly to the prospect.

In some cases, you won't be able to avoid speaking with the gatekeeper. When encountering a corporate gatekeeper, it is important that the gatekeeper knows who
you are and is confident that the purpose of your call would be welcomed by your prospect. Setting the gatekeeper at ease is essential. A corporate gatekeeper can be set at ease in much the same way you would set any prospect at ease.

Some points before making this call: Gatekeepers are just like any other human beings. They love to hear the sound of their own name and they rarely hear "thank you." Therefore we recommended you first learn the correct pronunciation of the gatekeeper's name. Think about this for a moment: Most gatekeepers pick up the phone and hear an unfamiliar voice on the other end asking for the boss. In a flash they spring into gatekeeper mode. Once on the defensive, not only do they want to know who you are and what you want, but they also want your life story and credit rating.

If you reach the prospect's voice mail first, leave a message saying that you will call again. Suggest to the prospect to inform the gatekeeper that you will be calling and that your call be allowed through. Even if he does not do this, you will differentiate yourself by the dialogue. Here's an example:

# CHAPTER TEN

Grant: *"Hello, Sue Smith? This is Grant Baker with Universal Supply Company calling for Jim — <u>he may have told you I would be calling</u>. Is he in? I only need a few moments."*

In this example, I greet the gatekeeper with both first and last name, differentiating this call from the countless others the gatekeeper receives on a daily basis. Also, because I
left a voice mail for my prospect saying that I would be calling and asking him to inform the gatekeeper about it, the greater the likelihood my call will be passed on unchallenged.

Domestic Gatekeeper
As with any call you make, applying the principles of STEER will guide you to a more effective strategy in getting past a gatekeeper. In dealing with a domestic gatekeeper, it is also important that they be set at ease before they will pass your call on to the prospect. Gatekeepers can shut you out with the same velocity as the prospects themselves, if not faster, as they may be even less familiar with you, your company and/or the referring individual than the prospects are. As we discussed earlier, differentiating yourself at hello is vital.

When requesting to speak your target prospect, it is important to speak with a relaxed yet confident tone, sounding as if you have had a relationship with the prospect for years. We suggest that you avoid formal prefixes such as Mr., Mrs., or Ms., as these are screaming red flags of unfamiliarity. Be brief and to the point, and immediately request that the gatekeeper summon the prospect for you. End your request with a "thank you," as this indicates the end of your request and is an assumption that the gatekeeper will follow through on your request.

For example:

"Hi, is Matt there? This is Mike Spencer calling; thanks..."

When calling on a referral, you can quickly set the gatekeeper at ease by establishing in the gatekeeper's mind that you are familiar with the prospect and that they would be delighted to take your call. State **up front** your association with the prospect, **then** state your name. By stating your association first, you immediately establish familiarity.

For example:

"Hello, I'm a friend of Paul Young. My name is Grant Baker. May I speak with Frank, please?"

If asked by the gatekeeper, "Who is Paul Young?", simply address the association with the information you wrote down when building your prospect list:

"Paul and Frank graduated from college together."

Since your goal is to pass the gatekeeper with minimal conversation, it is essential to have this information at your fingertips. It will prove well worth the effort.

A Few Words on Voice Mail
I (Grant) remember back in the early '80s when my company

installed voice mail in our office phone system. At first, I thought, *This is great. I'll never miss another call. My customers and prospects can just leave a voice message that I can save, transfer to another colleague, or just delete.* What a great idea! Then I realized that in addition to being a great message taker for me, a voice-mail system is also a great gatekeeper for my customers and prospects — one that is tough to get around.

I quickly learned that to get past voice mail, I needed some new strategies. A typical voice-mail system usually allows you to leave a quick message. If the message is compelling, you will likely get a return call. You may find that it will take several messages before your prospect calls you back. If the prospect never calls you back, don't worry; just move on down your list. Don't waste time worrying about someone who will not return your calls. Remember, it is a good idea to build and maintain a large prospect list; it makes moving on much easier. After all, if someone is determined never to answer the phone personally or return a call, neither I nor anyone else can change that.

A Few Tips on Leaving Voice-Mail Messages
A prospect's voice-mail system can sometimes work to your advantage. A well-constructed message left on your prospect's voice mail enables you to:

- Reach a prospect who is otherwise unreachable.
- Deliver your invitation for an appointment without objection or interruption.
- Make calls during off-hours, enabling you to fill otherwise unproductive time.

- Receive a return call, which is an invitation for you to speak live with a prospect who has now expressed an interest in speaking with you.

Components of an Effective Voice-Mail Message

A voice-mail script is similar to your previous scripts, with a few subtle exceptions. Let's build a sample voice-mail script.

Set the Prospect at Ease

Your voice may be unfamiliar to your prospect, so it is important that you take the time to set the prospect at ease through familiarity just like with all your other scripts.

"Hello Frank Smith, Grant Baker calling with Arnold Gregory & Associates — we are the IT consulting group that installed the CRM system at Second Niagara Credit Union."

Take Control

When you speak into a recording device, you may think you are in control, but remember, upon playback, your prospect can delete your message with a push of a single button. You need to establish control in such a way that compels the prospect to listen to your entire message. When leaving a message, don't be shy about saying that you want to speak to the prospect **live**. It is important that you make this known in your message. Here's an example:

"Frank, we just finished up our work at Second Niagara two weeks early and about $50,000 under budget — I'd like to speak directly with you to see if there is an opportunity to do similar work for Big Bucks University. I will call you back in an hour. Please let Joan

(Frank's administrative assistant) know that I will be calling, as I only need a moment of your time and won't mind holding for you if you are tied up on another call. If there is a better time to reach you, please let Joan know and I'll work my schedule accordingly."

In this example, there is some compelling information in just a few quick sentences. Frank "heard" that:

- Our company offers unique value that he may be interested in.
- We need to speak live. My merely leaving a message won't do.
- He can ask Joan, his administrative assistant, to expect my call, and tell her I am willing to wait on hold for a moment of his time.

Reaffirm After Confirming

Let your prospects know once again that you intend to call back at a specific time and on a specific day, and that you look forward to speaking with them soon:

"Frank, I look forward to speaking with you soon. I'll try back in about an hour."

Your prospect now knows that you called about something important, that you want to speak live, that it is important that you do speak, and that you intend to call back. He can speed the process along if he leaves a message with instructions as to how you can reach him directly.

Getting Down To It

OK, now it is time to start making your calls. You may begin to feel some butterflies in your stomach as you sit with your list. Even after years of practice, it is common for even skilled professionals to have their heart quicken and their palms sweat just before they pick up the phone. A little discomfort is not only normal but it also has its value. Having some nervous energy often means that you feel that what you are doing is important and that you care about being the best that you can be. Don't fight this energy — embrace it!

Visualization

In Chapter 2 we asked you to write down some compelling reasons why your prospects would want to meet with you. This is a good time to take a moment to review these reasons. For me (Grant), it was the value my company and equipment brought to my prospects, with value defined as:

- Better equipment reliability
- Better print-image quality
- Faster service

These advantages really made a positive difference to my customers. I was so convinced of these benefits that I was compelled to share them. Belief is a very powerful force — so powerful that it can compel action. Belief in your product, your company and the service you provide makes it easier to speak with confidence about how these advantages could benefit your prospects. However, you also need to get yourself psyched up just before sitting down to make prospecting calls. Here is how I did it then and how I continue to motivate myself today.

I always keep my prospecting materials together in a file folder. It's a kind of kit where I keep, no matter where I am, everything necessary to make calls. In this folder I have my prospect list, a clean pad of paper and my custom scripts. I also carry in my kit some special photographs as positive reminders. The purpose of these photographs is to remind me of what I am really working for and why I need to keep setting appointments. I have the latest pictures of my children, of a house that I cannot yet afford, and of my dream car (blue 1969 Dodge Charger R/T), as well as one other very important photograph.

This photograph reminds me of my very first in-person prospecting call. I walked into the crowded lobby of an office building on my first full day as a new sales rep. After asking who at the company made decisions on office printing equipment, the receptionist ordered me out of the lobby in front of what seemed to be a thousand people. I remember feeling defeated as I made it for the door with my head held low. Fortunately I recovered from this event. After that almost career-ending episode, I have learned how to use it as a powerful motivator. By photographing the front of that building and keeping the picture in my folder, it creates an "I'll show you" spirit in me. You need to find your own personal reminders that fuel your desires to achieve greater heights.

Before starting my calls, I place these pictures on the desk or table in a very specific order: first my children's pictures, followed by the home I can't afford yet, and then my dream car. I place the last picture — the front of that special office building — closest to me. You may think it sounds funny, but this symbolizes the barrier that almost ended my career.

It is essential that you believe in what you are calling about. However, belief alone may not be enough. I felt strongly that I represented a great company, with superior products and excellent service, before and after walking into that building. However, it was clear to me that belief alone was not enough to keep me going. I needed constant reminders of what I was willing to struggle for. Looking at the picture of that office building keeps fresh in my mind how silly it would be to let one rude person hold me back.

Do you have a strong, compelling reason to stay focused? Is it your family, your children, a certain goal you have always dreamed about? Great — get some pictures that represent what you want, what is important to you and what you are willing to struggle for. Place them in a folder and carry them with you at all times.

And one more thing: Recalling the false barrier that held that powerful Bengal Tiger at its mercy in chapter 1, get a small piece of cheesecloth and put that in with the pictures as well. Just before you make your calls, take out your prospecting kit and arrange these pictures on the desk or table in front of you. Now place the piece of cheesecloth in front of all that is important. The cheesecloth represents fear, hesitation and procrastination. Don't let this keep you from what you really want and what is really important to you. It looks kind of silly there, doesn't it? Do you think it can hold you back?

We didn't think so either.

"Come to the edge," he said.
They said, "We are afraid."
"Come to the edge," he said.
They came. He pushed them —
and they flew.

— GUILLAUME APOLLINAIRE

Summary

GOOD INTENTIONS AND $1.29 WILL BUY you a cup of coffee. All the ability, skill and enthusiasm are for naught without action. The fastest of vehicles stand still in neutral, even if the engine is running. Now is the time to put your machine in gear.

Dream vs. Fantasy

Having a crystallized dream is vital. You must have a compelling reason from within if you are going to go the extra mile, endure the uncomfortable and have the staying power to win. However, here's a word of caution — don't let your dreams turn into fantasies. A dream absent action quickly becomes a mere fantasy.

It feels great to imagine how wonderful it would be to be debt-free, purchase your dream home, take the vacations of your dreams, buy that perfect boat or retire early to that great cottage on the lake that you have been eyeing for years. Or maybe you envision yourself riding down the open road on your new Harley-Davidson (that's J.T.'s latest dream) or whatever it is that you're hoping, dreaming and working for. But remember that just thinking about it does not get the job done. You must put your new skills to work in order to make progress.

We are not saying that you should not keep your dreams in front of you. Writing them down, posting pictures on the refrigerator or even paying a visit to the local Mercedes-Benz dealership can help keep you focused. What we are saying is that you should get moving, consistently doing the productive activities that move business forward. At this point, *action* is now all that remains.

In our lines of work, there are only three productive activities. They are:

1. Setting appointments.
2. Presenting products and services.
3. Securing customer commitments.

That is it. Other activities may be important, but make no mistake — we do not confuse them with the real work that moves us closer to our goals. For us, the three activities above are daily business priorities and are at the top of every workday schedule.

What are the primary activities that will move your business forward? Turn to the last page of this book and write them down. You might want to tear the page out and keep it with you. Periodically stop what you are doing and look at the activity list you just made. Are you doing one of those activities now? If not, think about what you are doing, think about what you really want, and get moving.

Productive Activities

About the Authors:

R. Grant Baker

 Upon graduation from Rochester Institute of Technology in 1983, R. Grant Baker began his career with Eastman Kodak. Earning top sales honors, he progressed to marketing education specialist, sales manager, and worldwide product-line manager.

Mr. Baker expanded his career in direct sales, consulting for Oce' and Canon USA, and has conducted sales training programs for IBM, Heidelberg and Nexpress, LLC.

Currently, Mr. Baker is co-founder of Sales Boot Camp Inc., a consulting and sales training firm that develops and delivers customized skill-building programs designed to increase the effectiveness, profit potential and longevity of entrepreneurs and sales professionals.

About the Authors:

James Timothy (J.T.) Tasker

 After graduating from Buffalo State College, J.T. Tasker began his business career by co-founding CRA Seminars, an education company marketing a successful lecture series to colleges and universities throughout the northeastern United States. Mr. Tasker has since grown an international sales and marketing concern from start-up to annual revenues of $2.5 million.

Today Mr. Tasker coaches new and seasoned business owners alike with a focus on marketing and sales. He is also the co-founder of Sales-Boot Camp, Inc.